# THE ART OF SONG

A graded selection of songs
through the ages

## Grades 4–5

medium-low voice

ALLE RECHTE VORBEHALTEN · ALL RIGHTS RESERVED
**EDITION PETERS**
PUBLISHED BY FABER MUSIC
Leipzig · London · New York

Download accompaniment tracks and practice tracks by scanning the QR code or going to fabermusic.com/editionpetersresources.

Cover images (clockwise from top left): Around the Piano, Firle, Walther (1859–1929) / Waterhouse and Dodd, London, UK, / The Bridgeman Art Library; The Singing Lesson, 1882 (oil on canvas), Toulouse-Lautrec, Henri de (1864–1901) / Musee Toulouse-Lautrec, Albi, France, Lauros / Giraudon / The Bridgeman Art Library; Die Lautenspielerin, Borch d. J., Gerard ter (1617–1681); Schubert at the Piano, 1899 (oil on canvas), Klimt, Gustav (1862–1918); The Love Song, c. 1717 (oil on canvas), Watteau, Jean-Antoine (1684–1721); Les café-concert des Ambassadeurs, 1876/7 (pastel on montype), Degas, Edgar Germain Hilaire (1834–1917)

This edition © Copyright 2008 by Hinrichsen Edition, Peters Edition Limited, London

# CONTENTS

| | | |
|---|---|---|
| Arne | When daisies pied | 4 |
| Campion | The peaceful western wind | 6 |
| Ford | Since first I saw your face | 8 |
| Lully | Bois épais | 10 |
| Purcell | The Knotting Song | 12 |
| Purcell | Man is for the woman made | 13 |
| Purcell | Love quickly is pall'd | 14 |
| Scarlatti | O cessate di piagarmi | 16 |
| Brahms | Sandmännchen | 18 |
| Grieg | Jägerlied | 22 |
| Grieg | Med en Primula veris | 24 |
| Mozart | An die Freundschaft | 26 |
| Mozart | Die Zufriedenheit | 28 |
| Mozart | Die kleine Spinnerin | 30 |
| Schubert | Seligkeit | 33 |
| Schubert | Abendlied | 36 |
| Schubert | An die Laute | 38 |
| Schubert | Tischlerlied | 40 |
| Schumann | Die Waise | 43 |
| Sullivan | On a tree by a river | 44 |
| Anon. | Nina | 47 |
| Beethoven | Die Ehres Gottes aus der Natur | 50 |
| Campion | There is a garden in her face | 52 |
| Franck | Panis Angelicus | 54 |
| Arne | Where the bee sucks | 58 |
| Handel | Dove sei? | 61 |
| Haydn | Sailor's Song | 64 |
| Morley | It was a lover and his lass | 68 |
| Purcell | Fairest Isle | 70 |
| Handel | Where'er you walk | 72 |
| Grieg | Margretes Vuggesang | 75 |
| Brahms | Vergebliches Ständchen | 76 |
| Grieg | Jeg elsker Dig | 80 |
| Mozart | Die betrogene Welt | 82 |
| Schubert | An Sylvia | 86 |
| Grieg | Prinsessen | 90 |
| Schubert | Trauer der Liebe | 93 |
| Sullivan | The Willow Song | 96 |
| Sullivan | When a felon's not engaged in his employment | 100 |
| Sullivan | When a merry maiden marries | 102 |
| Schumann | Hinaus in's Freie! | 106 |

# When daisies pied

William Shakespeare (1564–1616)

Thomas Arne (1710–1778)

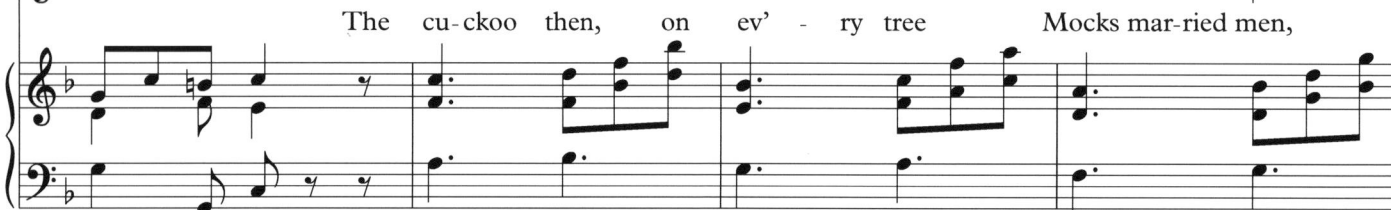

Edition Peters No. 71764
© Copyright 2008 by Hinrichsen Edition, Peters Edition Ltd, London

# The peaceful western wind

Thomas Campion (1567–1620)  
Thomas Campion (1567–1620)

range:

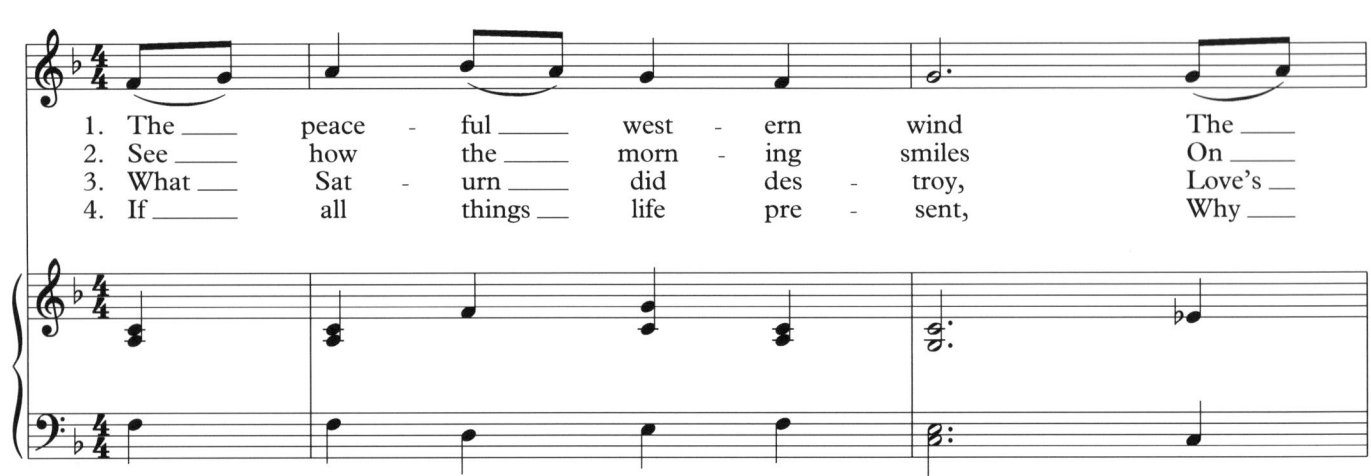

1. The peaceful western wind  The winter storms hath tamed;  And Nature in each kind  The kind heat hath inflamed.
2. See how the morning smiles  On her bright eastern hill;  And with soft steps beguiles  Them that lie slumbering still.
3. What Saturn did destroy,  Love's queen revives again;  And now her naked boy  Doth in the fields remain.
4. If all things life present,  Why die my comforts then?  Why suffers my content?  Am I the worst of men?

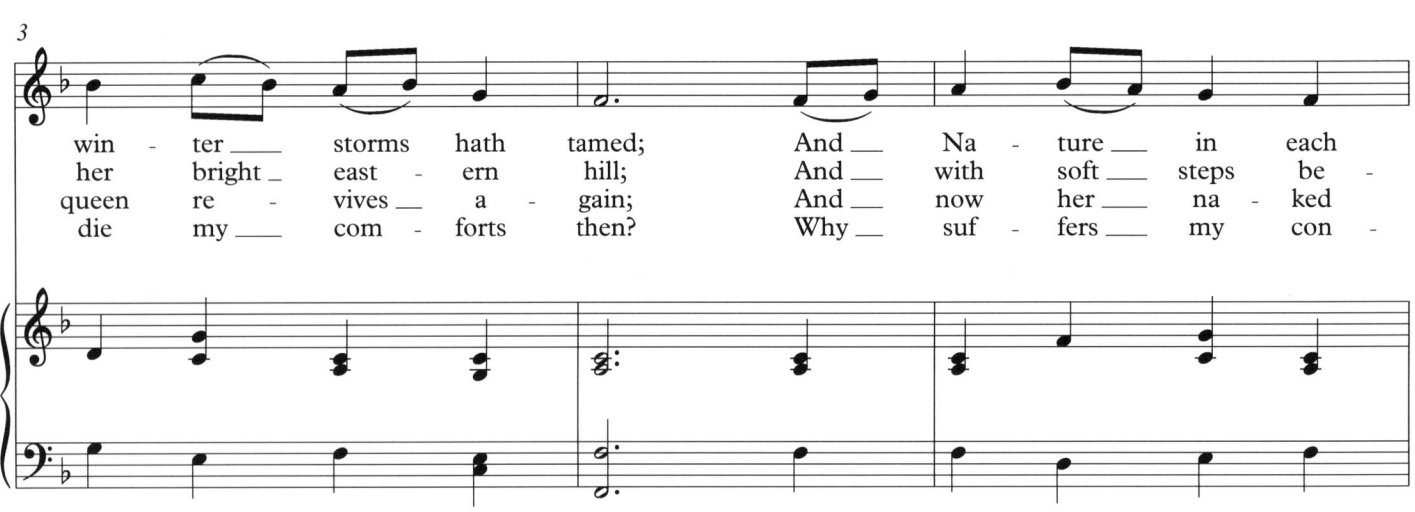

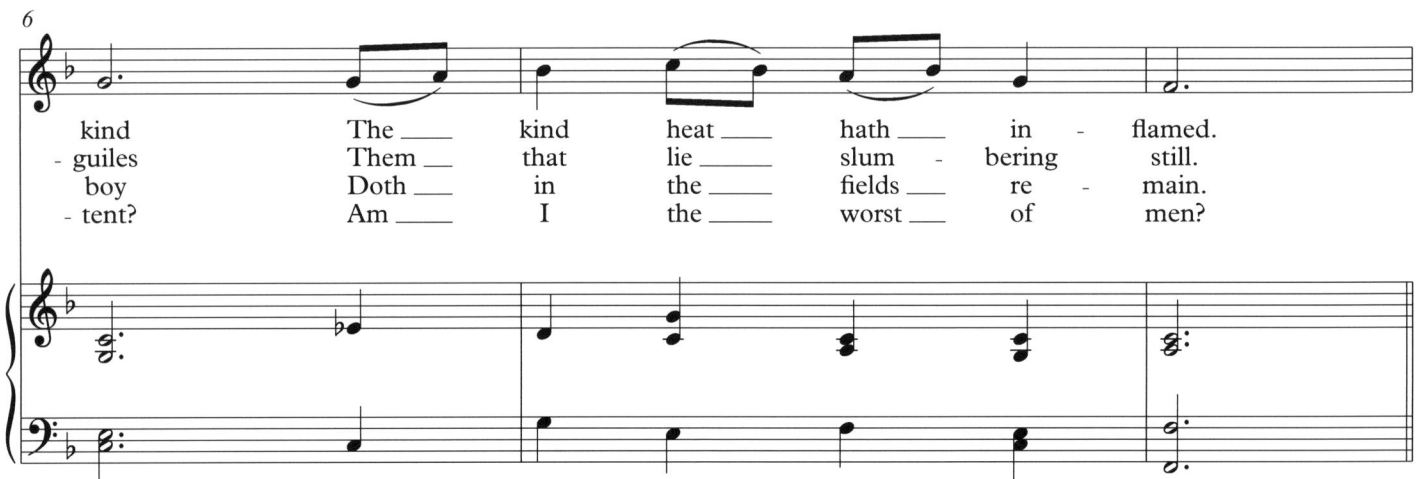

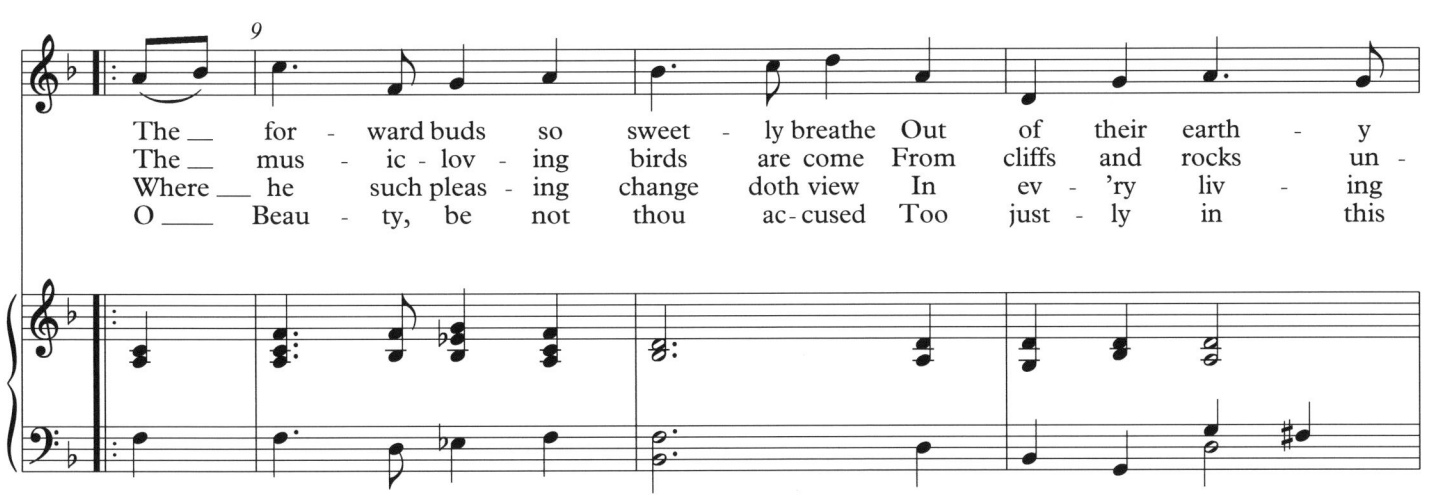

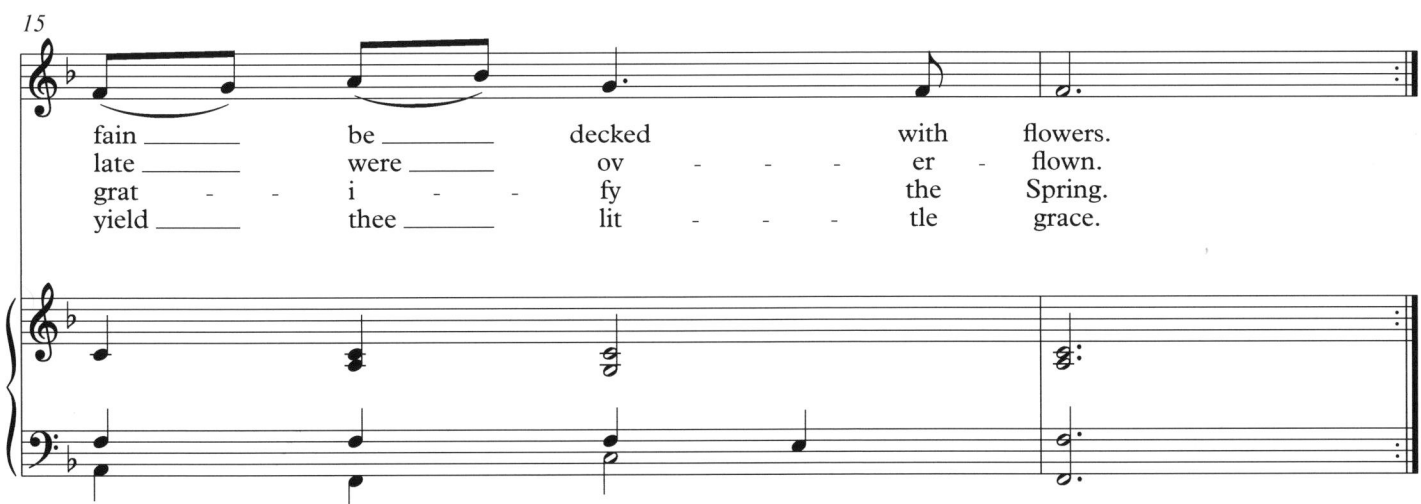

# Since first I saw your face

Anonymous

Thomas Ford (1580–1648)

range:

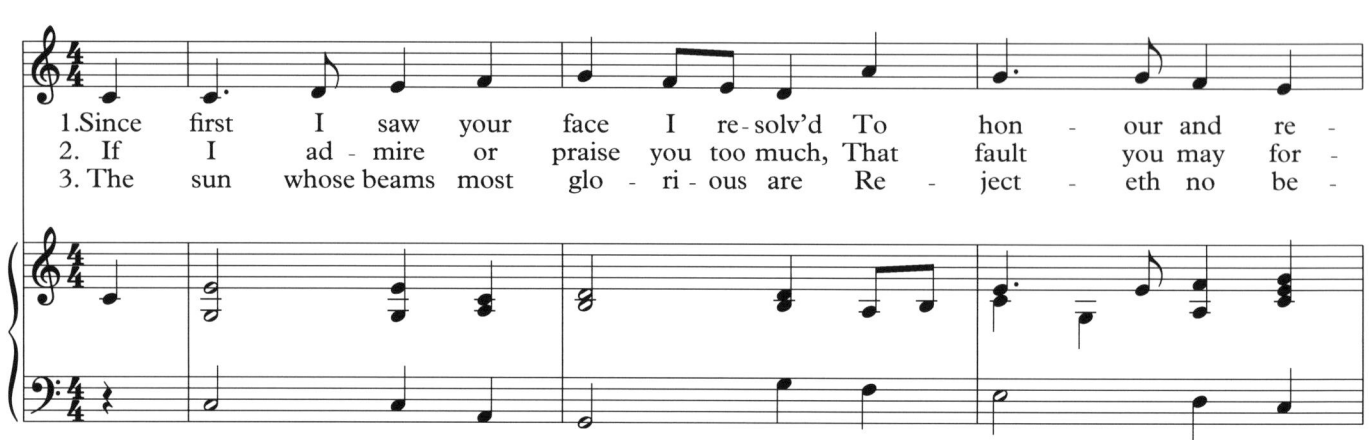

1. Since first I saw your face I re-solv'd To hon-our and re-nown ye. If now I be dis-dain-ed I wish My heart had nev-er known ye. What, I that lov'd and

2. If I ad-mire or praise you too much, That fault you may for-give me. Or if my hands had stray'd but a touch, Then just-ly might you leave me. I ask'd you leave, you

3. The sun whose beams most glo-ri-ous are Re-ject-eth no be-hold-er; And your sweet beau-ty past com-pare Made my poor eyes the bold-er. Where Beau-ty moves and

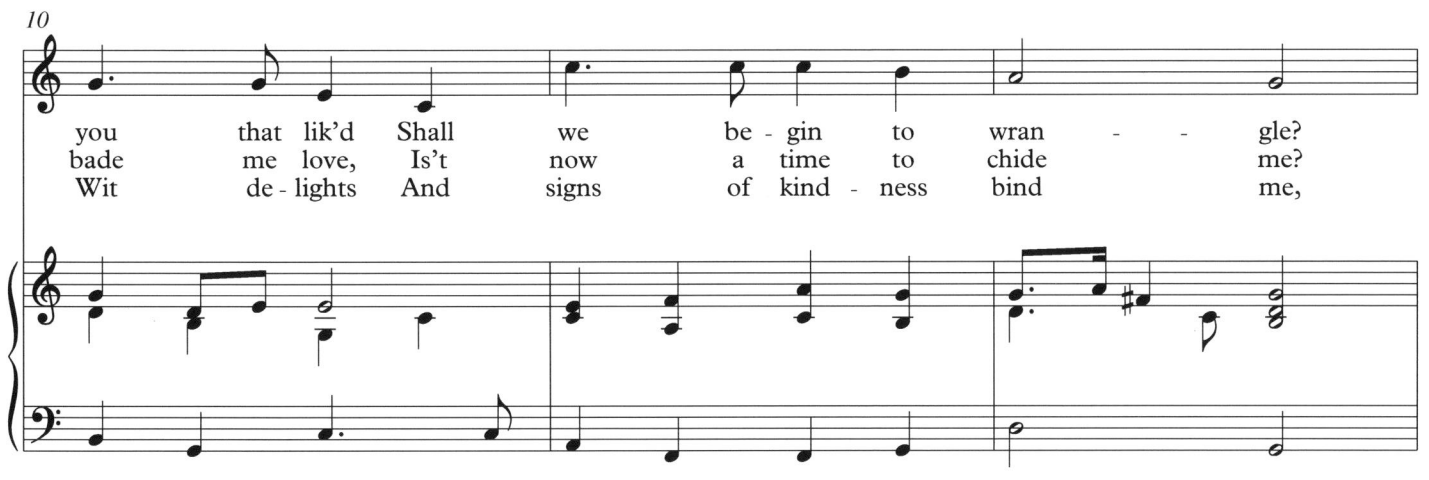

# Bois épais
*Cast your shade*

Philippe Quinault (1635–1688)  
Jean-Baptiste Lully (1632–1687)

range:

# The Knotting Song

Sir Charles Sedley (1639–1701)  
Henry Purcell (1659–1695)

range:

**[Allegretto]**

1. "Hears not my Phillis how the birds, Their feather'd mates salute? They tell their passion in their words, Must I alone, must I alone be mute?"
2. "The God of love in thy bright eyes Does like a tyrant reign; But in thy heart a child he lies, Without his dart, without his dart or flame."
3. "So many months in silence past, And yet in raging love, Might well deserve one word at last, My passion, my passion should approve."
4. "Must then your faithful swain expire, and not one look obtain, Which he to soothe his fond desire, Might pleasingly, might pleasingly explain?"

Phillis, without a frown or smile, Sat and knotted, and knotted, and knotted, and knotted all the while.

# Man is for the woman made

from *The Mock Marriage*

Peter Anthony Motteux (1663–1718)

Henry Purcell (1659–1695)

Man, man, man is for the woman made, And the woman made for man.

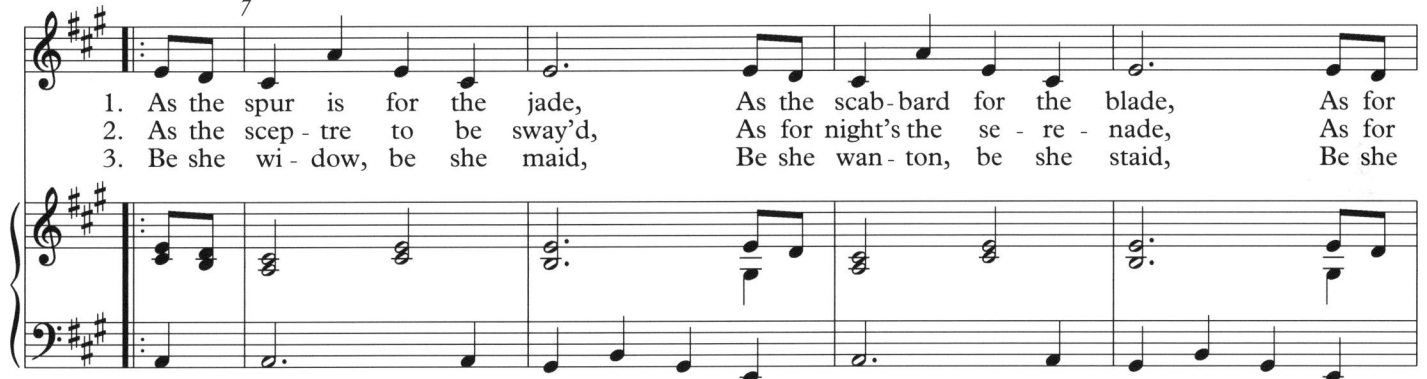

1. As the spur is for the jade, As the scabbard for the blade, As for
2. As the sceptre to be sway'd, As for night's the serenade, As for
3. Be she widow, be she maid, Be she wanton, be she staid, Be she

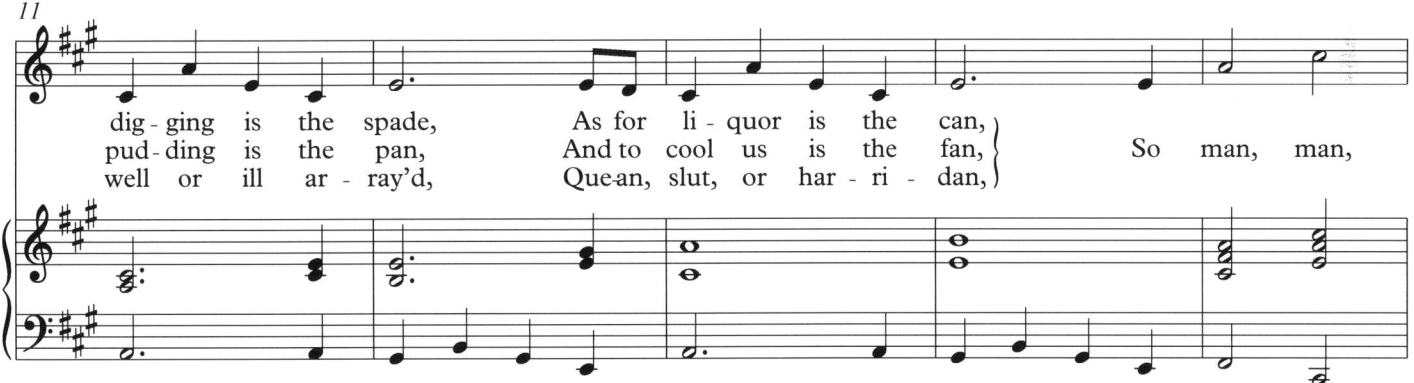

digging is the spade, As for liquor is the can,
pudding is the pan, And to cool us is the fan,  } So man, man,
well or ill array'd, Quean, slut, or harridan,

man is for the woman made, And the woman for the man.

# Love quickly is pall'd

Thomas Shadwell (1640–1692)

Henry Purcell (1659–1695)

range:

**[Vivace]**

Love quick-ly is pall'd, tho' with la-bour 'tis gain'd; Wine nev-er does cloy, no, nev-er does cloy, tho' with ease, with ease 'tis ob-tain'd. We sing, we sing while you sigh,

# O cessate di piagarmi
*Oh release me from this anguish*

Nicolò Minato (*c.* 1627–1698)  
Alessandro Scarlatti (1660–1725)

range:

1. O cessate di piagarmi, O lasciatemi morir,
2. Più d'un angue, più d'un aspe Crudi e sordi a miei sospir,
1. *Oh release me from this anguish, leave me here alone to die,*
2. *Crueler far than asp or serpent, deaf to your poor lover's sigh,*

O lasciatemi morir! Luci ingrate, dispietate,  
Crudi e sordi a miei sospir. Occhi alteri, ciechi e fieri,  
*leave me here alone to die! Eyes ungrateful, cold and hateful,*  
*deaf to your poor lover's sigh, proud, unyielding, void of feeling,*

# Sandmännchen
*The Little Sandman*

Anton Wilhelm Florentin von Zuccalmaglio (1803–1869)

Johannes Brahms (1833–1897)

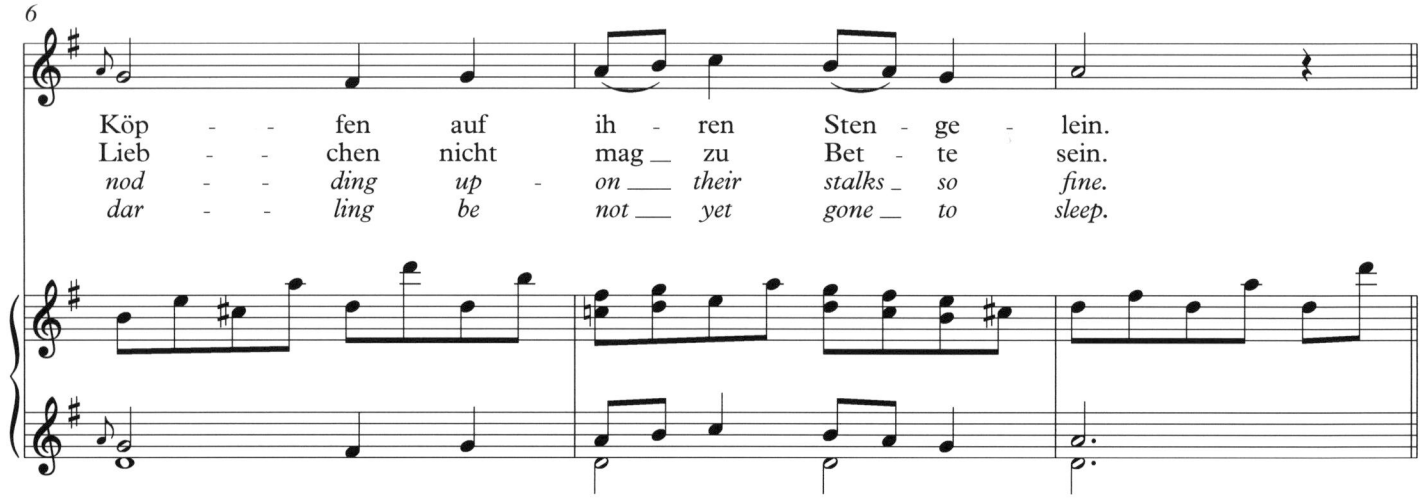

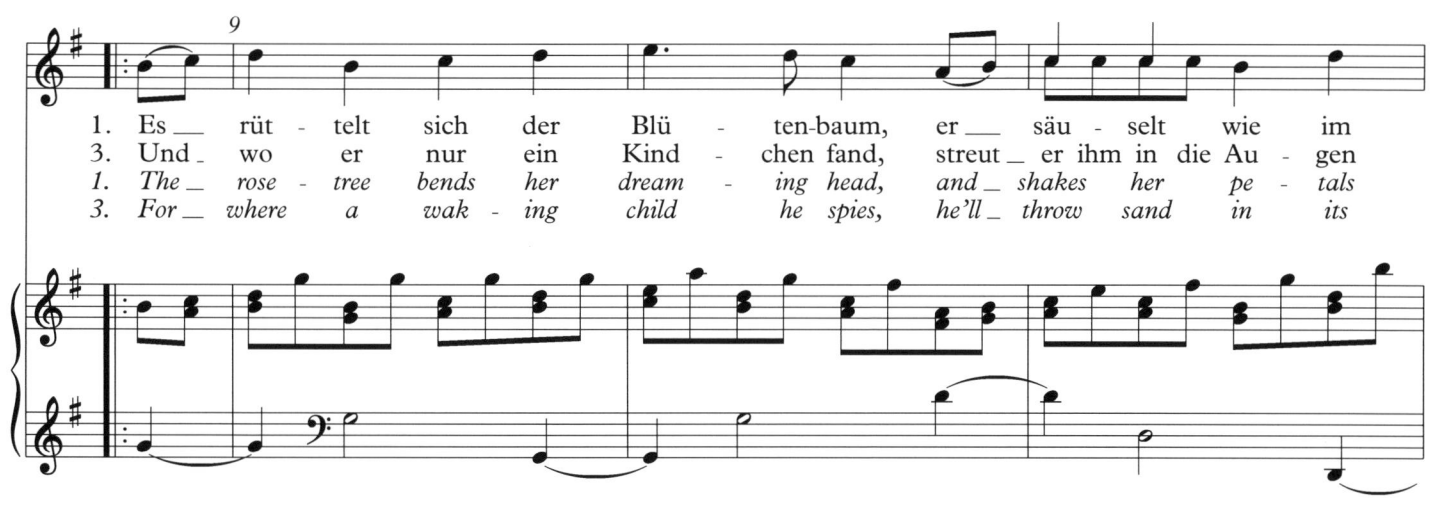

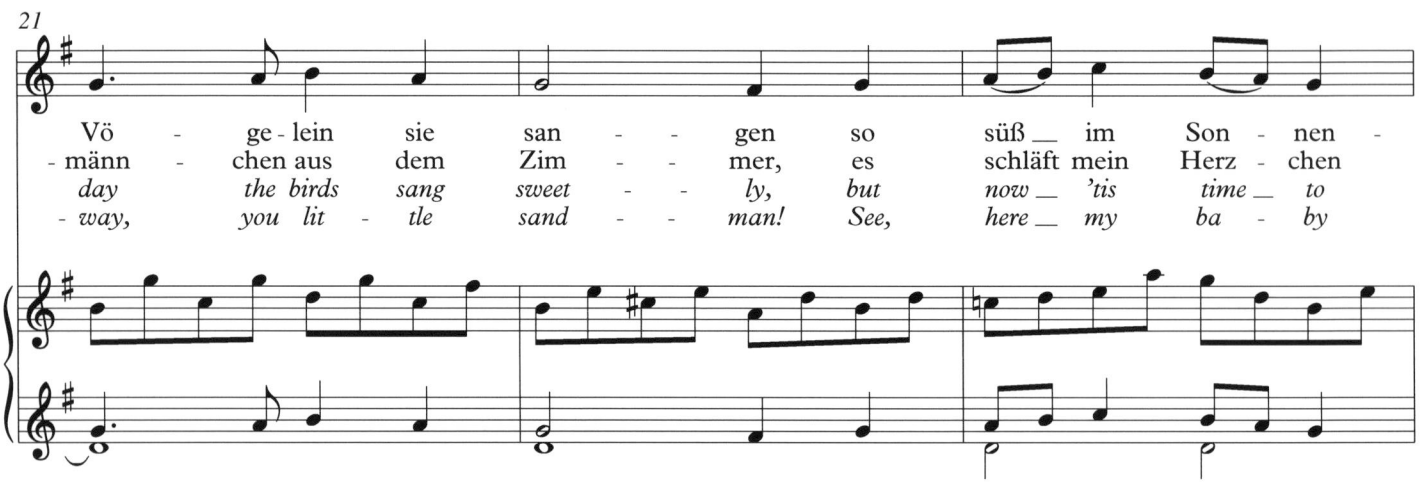

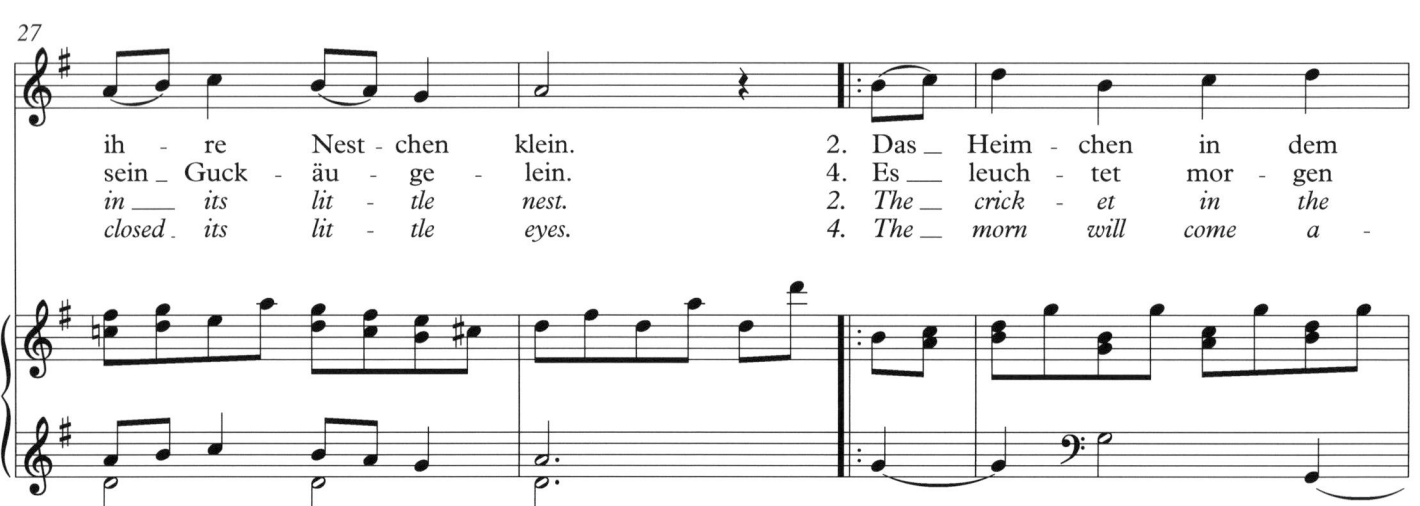

# Jägerlied / Jægersang
## Hunting Song

Ludwig Uhland (1787–1862)  
Edvard Grieg (1843–1907)

range:

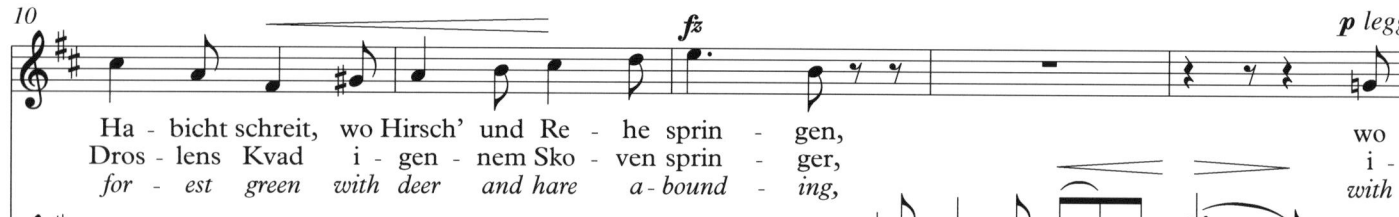

★ The octave leap upwards only applies to the Danish text when singing the higher variant.

# Med en Primula veris
# Mit einer Primula veris
*With a Primrose*

range:

John Olaf Paulsen (1851–1924)  
Edvard Grieg (1843–1907)

# An die Freundschaft
## To Friendship

Ludwig Friedrich Lenz (1717–1780)

Wolfgang Amadeus Mozart (1756–1791)

range:

**Langsam**

1. O heiliger Bund, dir weih ich meine Lieder, du höchstes Glück und Edens Wonne gleich! In deine Kreise zieht michs immer wieder, du machst das Leben schön und wonnereich, ja, das Leben schön und wonnereich.

2. Wie glücklich ist, wer hier auf diesen Welten, wo stets das Böse war des Guten Feind, und wo man treue Freundschaft findet selten, am Herzen ruhn kann einem treuen Freund, ja, am Herzen ruhn kann einem treuen Freund.

1. *To thee, sacred bond, I dedicate my praises, oh friendship fount of heav'nly peace and joy! Within the clasp of thy profound embraces there lies a beauty time cannot alloy, yes, a beauty time cannot alloy.*

2. *Oh happy man who, in this world of anguish, where good and evil fight until the end, and where true friendship ever seems to languish, can know the value of a faithful friend, yes, can know the value of a faithful friend.*

# Die Zufriedenheit
*Happiness*

Christian Felix Weiße (1726–1804)  
Wolfgang Amadeus Mozart (1756–1791)

range:

**(Andantino)**

1. Wie sanft, wie ruhig fühl ich hier des Lebens Freuden ohne Sorgen! und sonder Ahnung leuchtet mir will-
2. Wie sehr lach ich die Großen aus, die Blutvergießer, Helden, Prinzen! denn mich beglückt ein kleines Haus, sie

*1. How calm I feel, how peaceful here: the joys of life are mine to measure! For ev'ry day without a care I*
*2. How men of substance make me laugh, the kings and queens and their relations! For me this house is quite enough, yet*

# Die kleine Spinnerin
*The Little Spinner Girl*

Anonymous  
Wolfgang Amadeus Mozart (1756–1791)

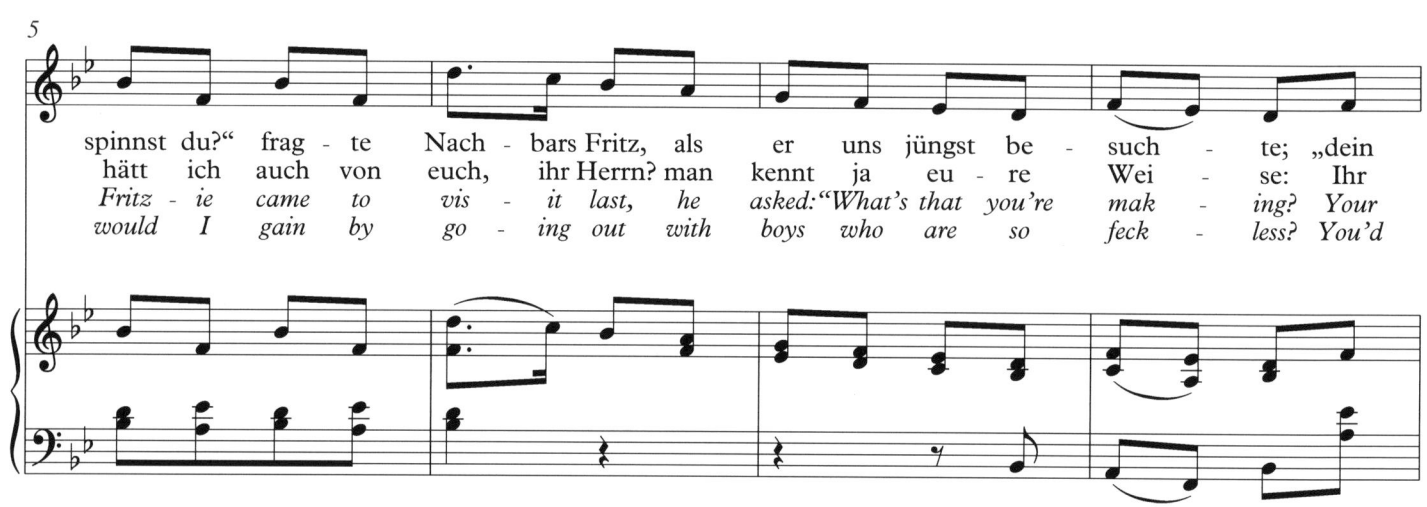

33

range:

# Seligkeit
*Heavenly Bliss*

Ludwig Heinrich Christoph Hölty (1748–1776)　　　　　　　　　　　　　　　　　Franz Schubert (1797–1828)

**Lustig**

1. Freu - den son - der Zahl blühn im Him - mels - saal
2. Je - dem lä - chelt traut ei - ne Him - mels - braut;
*1. Joys and per - fect love Fill the halls a - bove*
*2. There on ev - 'ry side Smiles a hea - ven - ly bride*

En - geln und Ver - klär - ten, wie die Vä - ter
Harf' und Psal - ter klin - get, und man tanzt und
*Bles - sed souls sur - round us, An - gels stand a -*
*Harp and cym - bals ring - ing, bles - sed spi - rits*

# Abendlied
## *Evening Song*

Matthias Claudius (1740–1815)

Franz Schubert (1797–1828)

range:

**Ruhig**

1. Der Mond ist auf - ge - gan - gen; die gold - nen Stern - lein
2. Wie ist die Welt so stil - le, und in der Dämm - rung

*1. A sil - ver moon is ris - ing; the stars like dia - monds*
*2. The world has grown so qui - et, and in the gen - tle*

pran - gen am Him - mel hell und klar; der Wald steht schwarz und
Hül - le so trau - lich und so hold! als ei - ne stil - le

*blaz - ing shall fill the sky with light; the wood is wreath'd in*
*twi - light, so wel - com - ing and kind, as if a sec - ret*

schwei - get, und aus den Wie - sen stei - get der weis - se Ne - bel
Kam - mer, wo ihr des Ta - ges Jam - mer ver - schla - fen und ver -

*sha - dow; a mist en - shrouds the mea - dow to greet the won - der*
*cham - ber where no one could re - mem - ber the dai - ly cares he*

wun - der - bar.
- ges - sen sollt.
*of the night.*
*left be - hind.*

# An die Laute
## To the Lute

Friedrich Rochlitz (1769–1842)  
Franz Schubert (1797–1828)

# Tischlerlied
## *The Carpenter's Song*

Anonymous  
Franz Schubert (1797–1828)

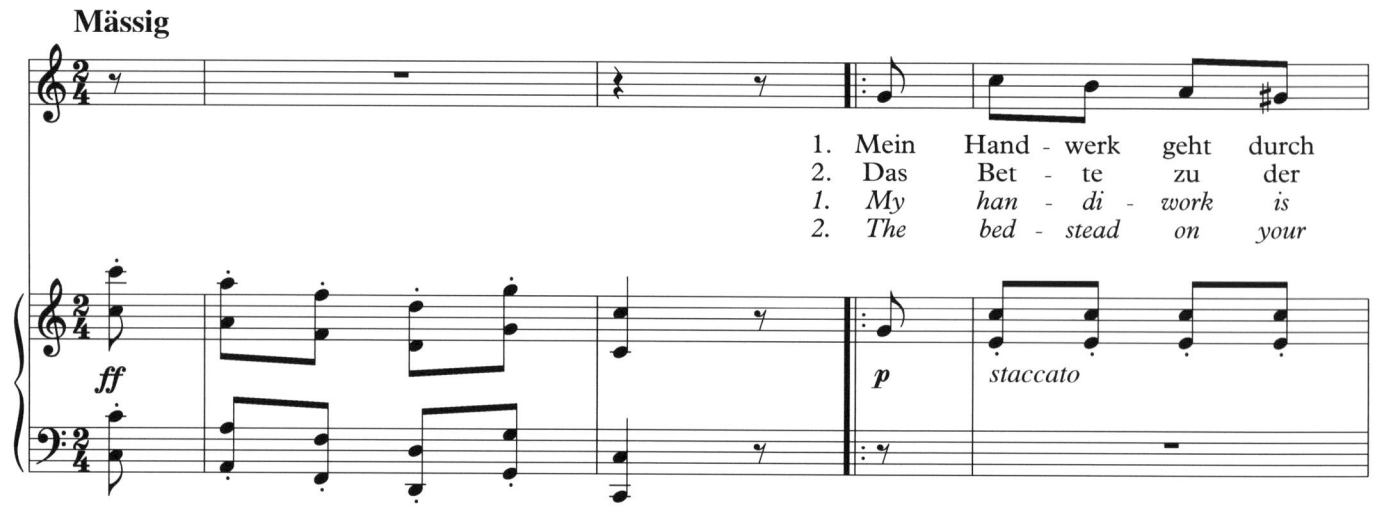

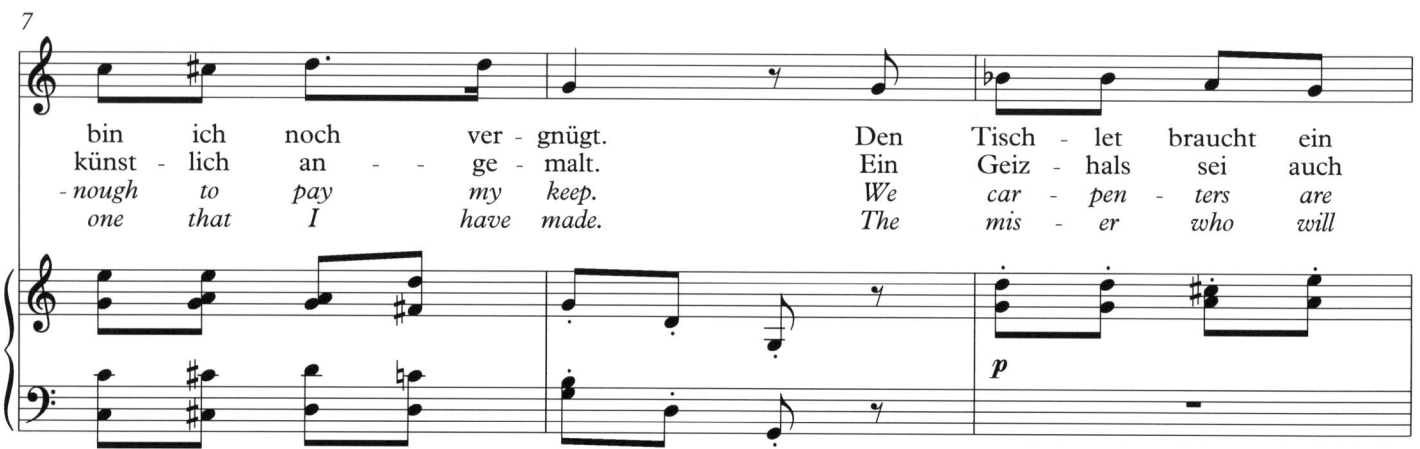

44

# On a tree by a river (Willow, Tit-willow)
## from *The Mikado*

W. S. Gilbert (1836–1911)

Arthur Sullivan (1842–1900)

range:

**Andante espressivo**

KO-KO

1. On a tree by a ri-ver a lit-tle tom-tit Sang "Wil-low, tit-wil-low, tit-wil-low!" And I said to him, "Dick-y-bird, why do you sit Sing-ing 'Wil-low, tit-wil-low tit-wil-low'? Is it weak-ness of in-tel-lect, bir-die?" I cried, "Or a ra-ther tough worm in your lit-tle in-side?" With a shake of his poor lit-tle head he re-plied, "Oh

range:

# Nina

Anonymous

Anon. Italian (attrib. Pergolesi)

[Andantino]

# Die Ehre Gottes aus der Natur
## *All Nature Sings God's Praises* ★

Christian Fürchtegott Gellert (1715–1769) — Ludwig van Beethoven (1770–1827)

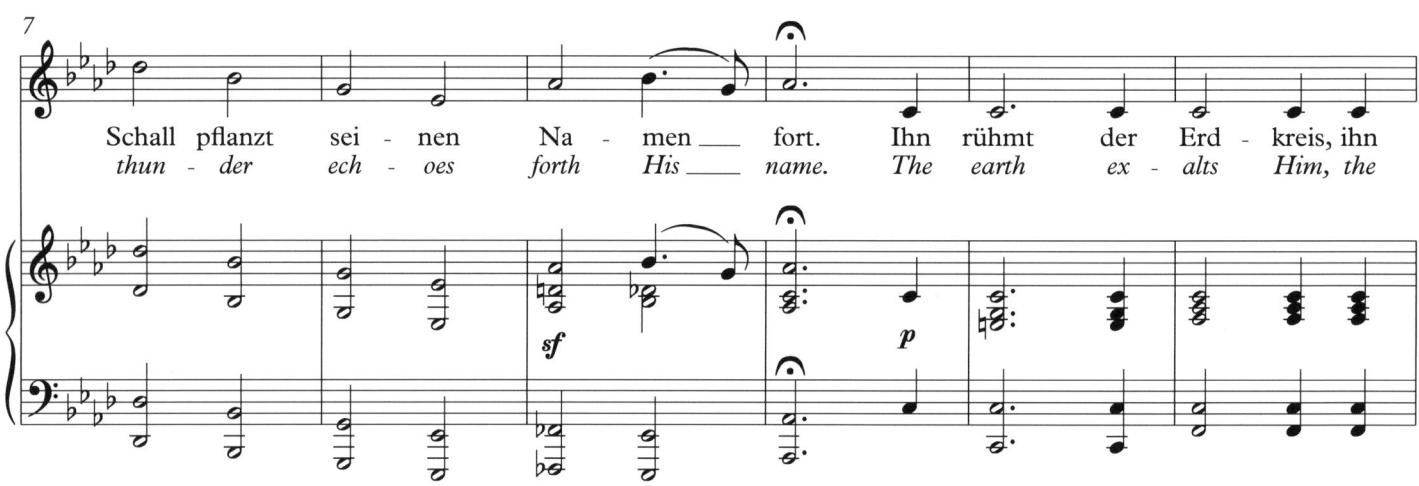

★ English text © 1994 by Frederick Fuller. Reproduced by permission of the translator.

# There is a garden in her face

Thomas Campion (1567–1620)  Thomas Campion (1567–1620)

1. There is a gar - den in her face,
2. Those cher - ries fair - ly do en - close
3. Her eyes like an - gels watch them still;

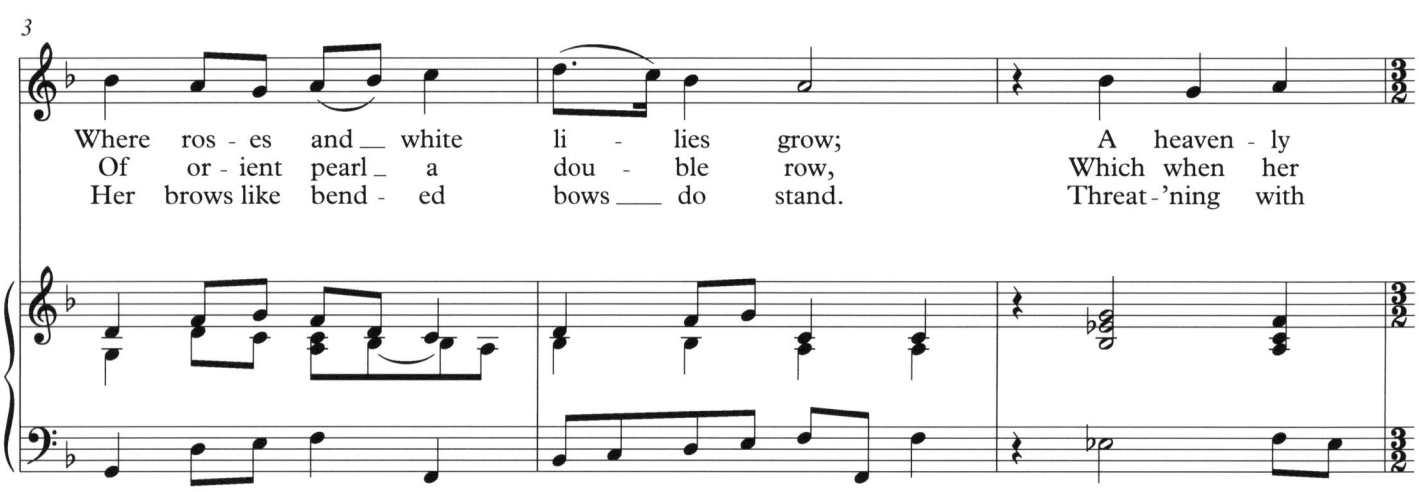

Where ros - es and white li - lies grow; A heaven - ly
Of or - ient pearl a dou - ble row, Which when her
Her brows like bend - ed bows do stand. Threat -'ning with

pa - ra - dise is that place, Where - in all plea - sant fruits do
love - ly laugh - ter shows, They look like rose - buds filled with
pier - cing frowns to kill All that at - tempt with eye or

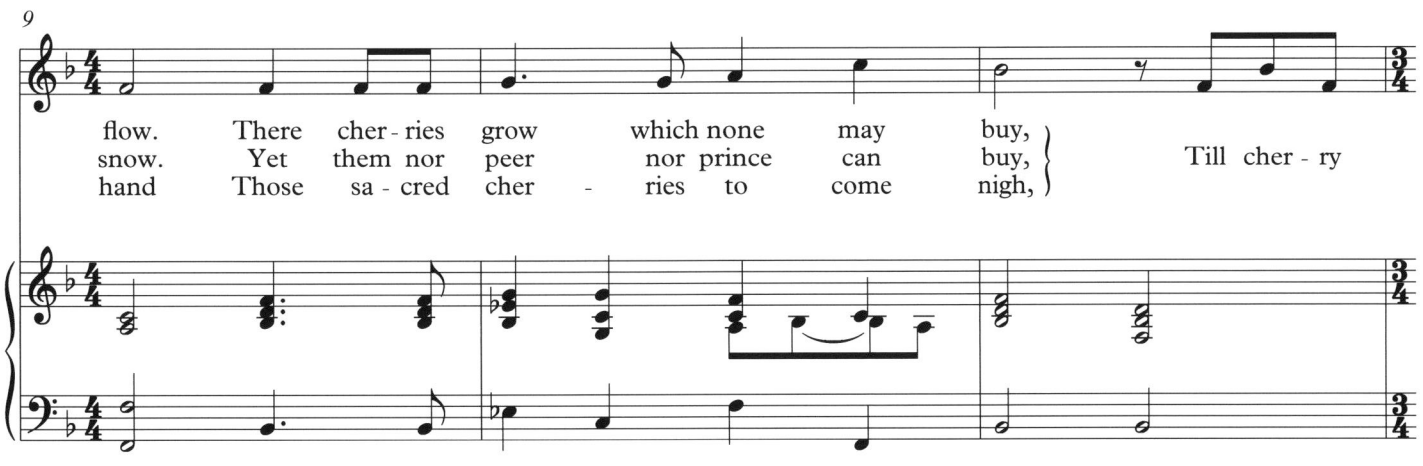

54

# Panis Angelicus
*Bread of the Sacrament*

Saint Thomas Aquinas (*c.* 1225–1274)

César Franck (1822–1890)

range:

**Poco lento**

**13** *dolce*

Pa — nis an — ge — li-cus   Fit pa — nis ho — mi-num
*Bread of the sac — ra-ment,   bread of hu — ma — ni - ty,*

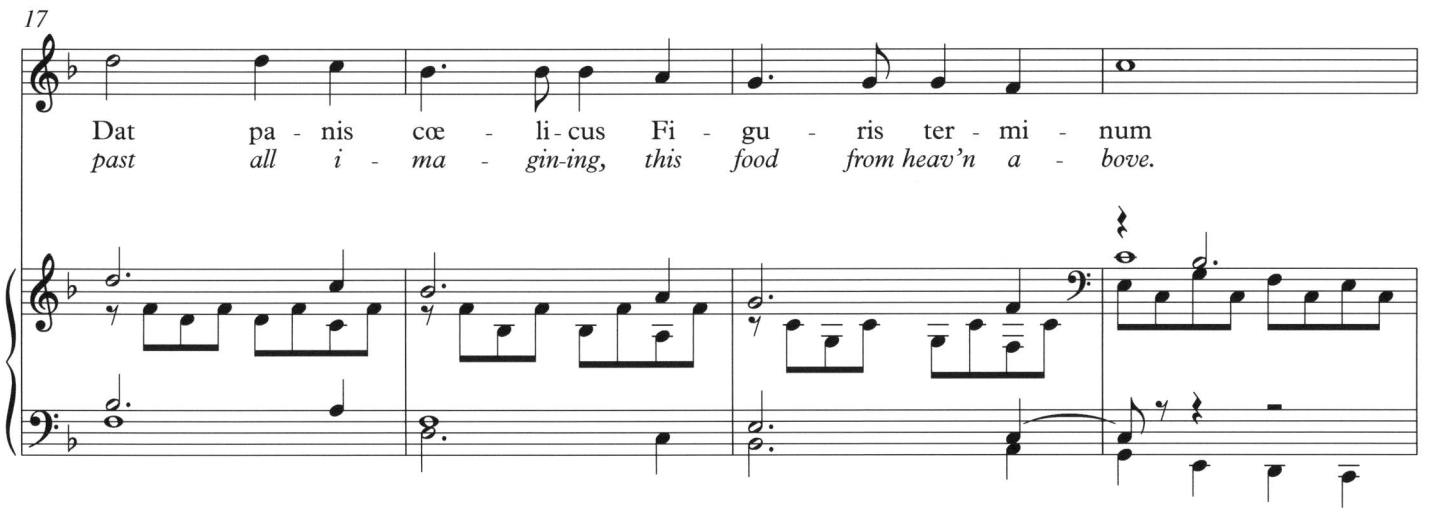

58

# Where the bee sucks

William Shakespeare (1564–1616)

Thomas Arne (1710–1778)

range:

**[Andante]**

Where the bee sucks, there suck I; In a cow-slip's bell I lie: There I

# Dove sei?
*Can you hear me?*

Nicola Francesco Haym (1678–1729)          George Frideric Handel (1685–1759)

range:

# Sailor's Song

Anonymous

Joseph Haydn (1732–1809)

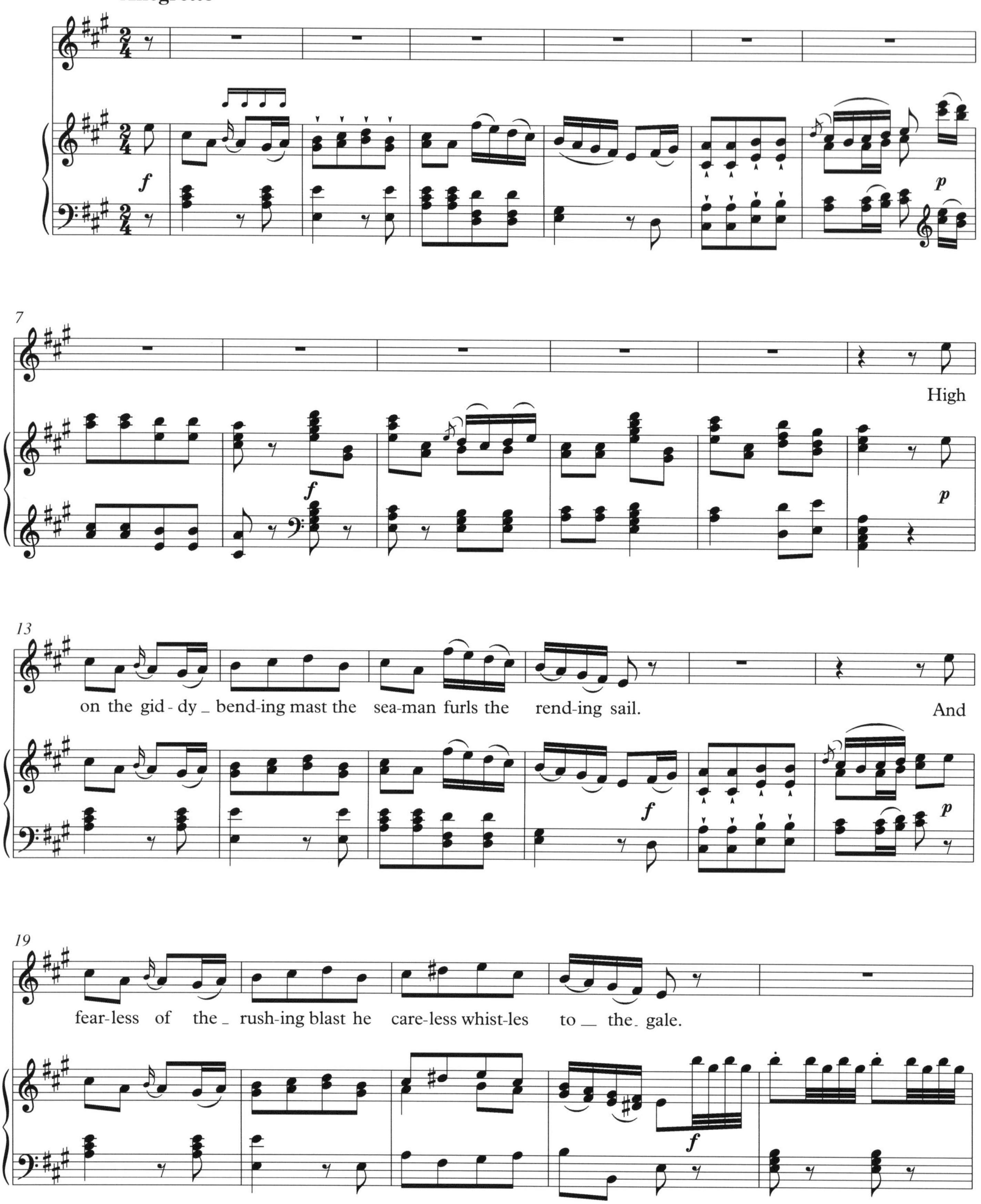
Allegretto
f
p
7
High
f
p
13
on the gid - dy _ bend-ing mast the sea-man furls the rend-ing sail.
And
f
p
19
fear-less of the _ rush-ing blast he care-less whist-les to _ the_ gale.
f

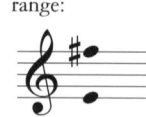

# It was a lover and his lass

William Shakespeare (1564–1616)  
Thomas Morley (1557–1602)

range:

1. It was a lov-er and his lass,
2. Be-tween the a-cres of the rye,
3. This ca-rol they be-gan that hour,
4. Then pret-ty lov-ers take the time,

With a hey, with a ho and a hey no-nie no, and a hey no-nie no-nie no,

1. That o'er the green corn-fields did pass,
2. These pret-ty coun-try fools would lie,
3. How that a life was but a flower,
4. For love is crown-ed with the prime,

In Spring time, in Spring time, in Spring time, the on-ly pret-ty ring time, When

# Fairest Isle
## (Address to Britain)
### from *King Arthur*

range:

John Dryden (1631–1700)  
Henry Purcell (1659–1695)

1. Fair-est isle, all isles ex-cel-ling,
2. Gen-tle mur-murs, sweet com-plain-ing,

Seat of plea-sure and of love  
Sighs that blow the fire of love

Ve-nus here will choose her dwell-ing,  
Soft re-pul-ses, kind dis-dain-ing,

And for-sake her Cy-prian grove.  
Shall be all the pains, you prove.

# Where'er you walk

William Congreve (1670–1729)

George Frideric Handel (1685–1759)

range:

[Largo e pianissimo]

# Margretes Vuggesang / Margaretens Wiegenlied
## Margaret's Cradle Song

Henrik Ibsen (1828–1906) — Edvard Grieg (1843–1907)

**Andante molto tranquillo**

Nu løf - tes Laft og Lof - te til Stjer - ne-hvæl-ven blaa, nu fly - ver lil - le Haa-kon med Drøm-me-vin-ger paa. Der er en Sti-ge stil - let fra Jord til Him-mel op, nu sti - ger lil - le Haa - kon med Eng - le - ne til top. Guds Eng - le smaa de vaa - ge for Vug - ge-bar-nets Fred, Gud sign dig, lil - le Haa-kon, din Mo-der vaa - ger med!

Nun schloß die Äug-lein bei - de zum Schlaf klein Ha-kon kaum, da sieht er schon mit La-chen den al - ler-schön-sten Traum. Es baut sich ei - ne Stie-ge hin - auf zum Him-mels-zelt, drauf stei - gen Got-tes Eng - lein her - nie - der zu der Welt. Die hü - ten sei - nen Schlum-mer ge - treu die gan - ze Nacht, schlaf süß und sanft, klein Ha - kon, auch dei - ne Mut - ter wacht.

*Now ri - ses roof and raf - ter to star - ry vaults of blue; now flies my litt - le Haa-kon on wings of dream-ing too. There climbs a lad-der lead-ing from earth to heav'n on high; now climbs my litt - le Haa - kon with an - gel-spi-rits nigh. God's che - ru-bims are watch-ing that babes may slum - ber true; God bless you, litt - le Haa - kon, your mo-ther wat - ches too.*

# Vergebliches Ständchen

*Fruitless Serenade* *

Anton Wilhelm Florentin von Zuccalmaglio (1803–1869)

Johannes Brahms (1833–1897)

range:

**Lebhaft und gut gelaunt**

(Er) Gu-ten A-bend, mein Schatz, gu-ten A-bend, mein Kind, gu-ten A-bend, mein Kind! Ich komm' aus Lieb' zu dir, ach, mach' mir auf die Tür, mach' mir auf die Tür, mach' mir auf, mach' mir auf, mach' mir auf die Tür!

*(He) Here I am be-neath your win-dow dea-rest, bear my se-re-nade, list-en to my se-re-nade. 'Tis true love brings me here, o-pen your door, my dear, let me in my sweet, let me in, let me in, let me in, my sweet!*

★ English text © 1994 by Frederick Fuller. Reproduced by permission of the translator.

# Jeg elsker Dig

# Ich liebe dich

*I love but thee*

Hans Christian Andersen (1805–1875)

Edvard Grieg (1843–1907)

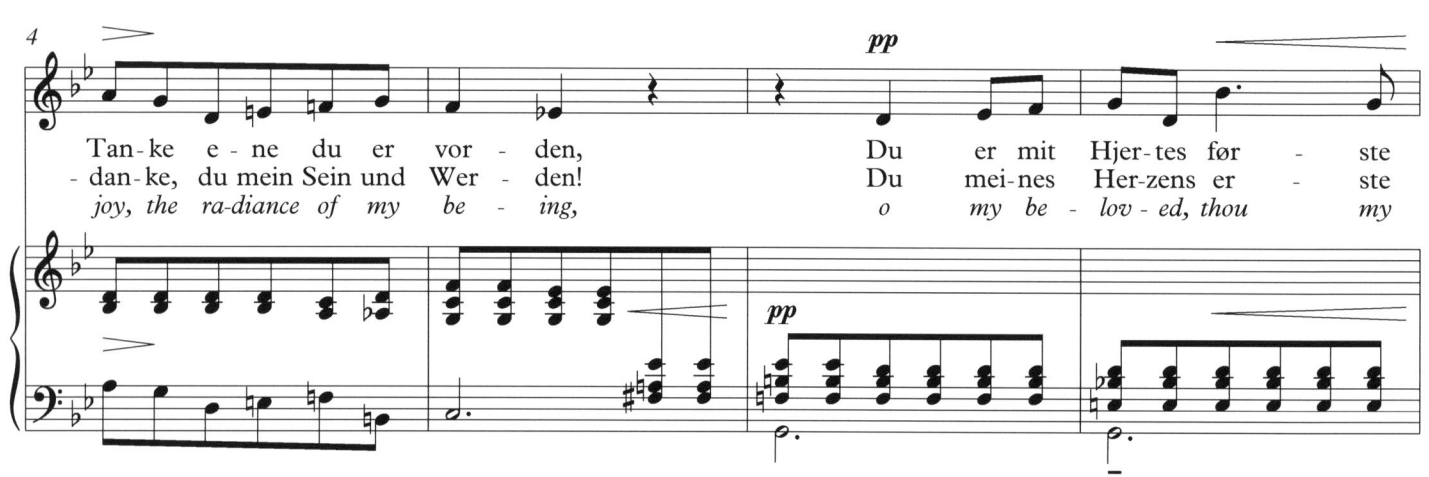

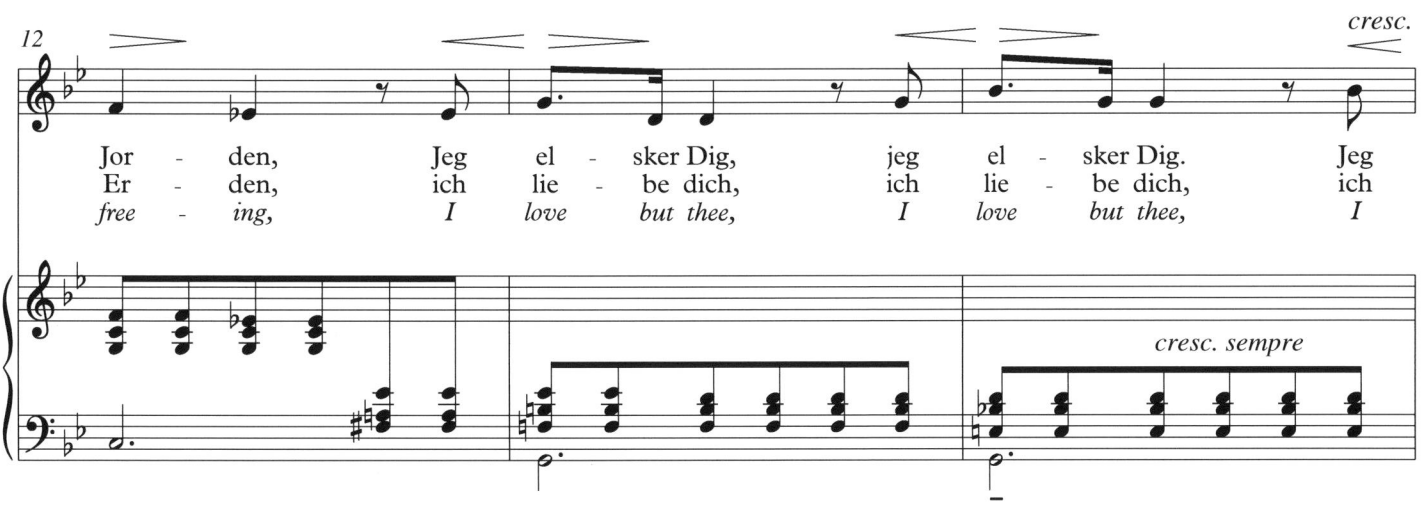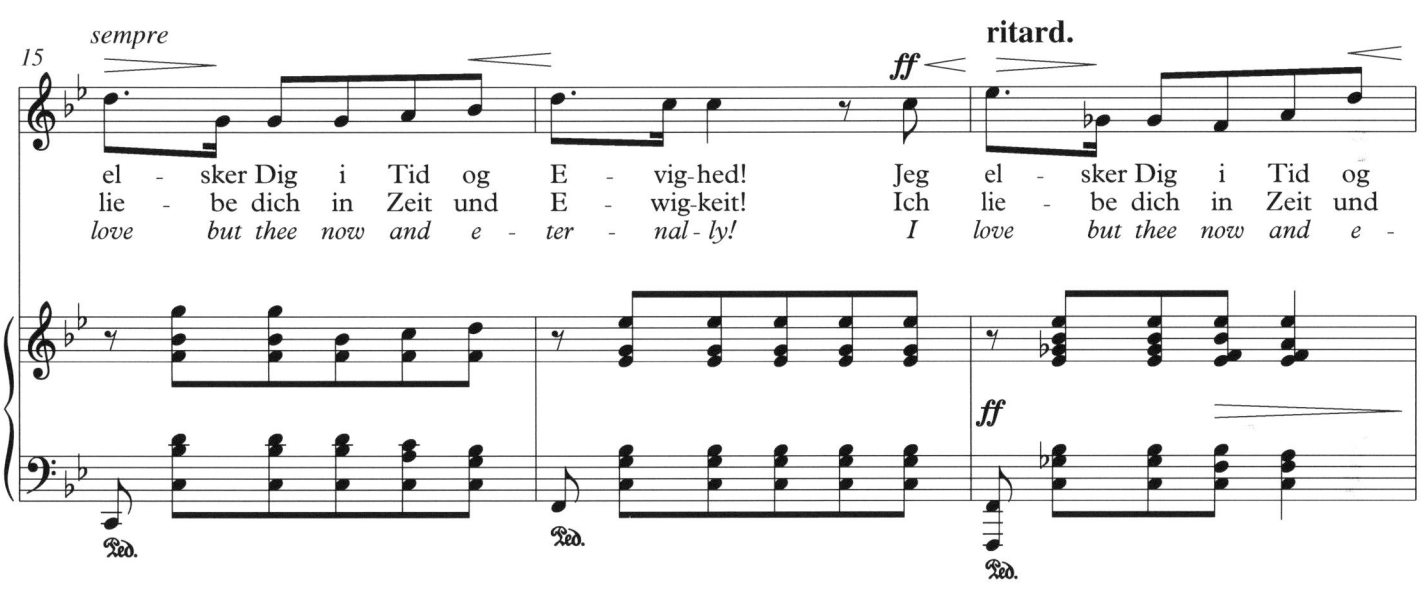

# Die betrogene Welt
## *The Deceiving World*

Christian Felix Weiße (1726–1804)  
Wolfgang Amadeus Mozart (1756–1791)

1. Der rei - che Tor, mit Gold ge-schmü-cket, zieht Se - li - me-nens Au-gen
2. Be - a - te, die vor we - nig Ta - gen der Buh - le - rin-nen Kro-ne
1. *A rich buf-foon whose brains are lack - ing has turned poor Mar-ga - ri - ta's*
2. *Suz-anne, in mem-or - y quite re - cent, would go with a - ny man who'd*

an, der wack - re Mann wird fort-ge-schi-cket, den Stut - zer wählt sie sich zum  
war, fängt an, sich vi - o - lett zu tra-gen, und klei - det Kan - zel und Al -  
*head: her wor - thy suit - or she sent pack-ing and wed the preen-ing fool in -*  
*pay; but now her clothes are plain and de - cent; she spends her time in church all*

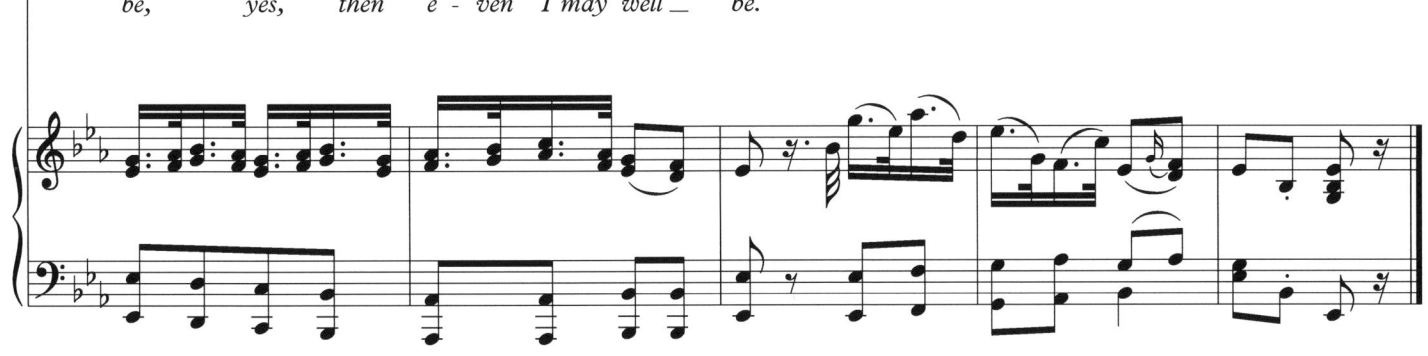

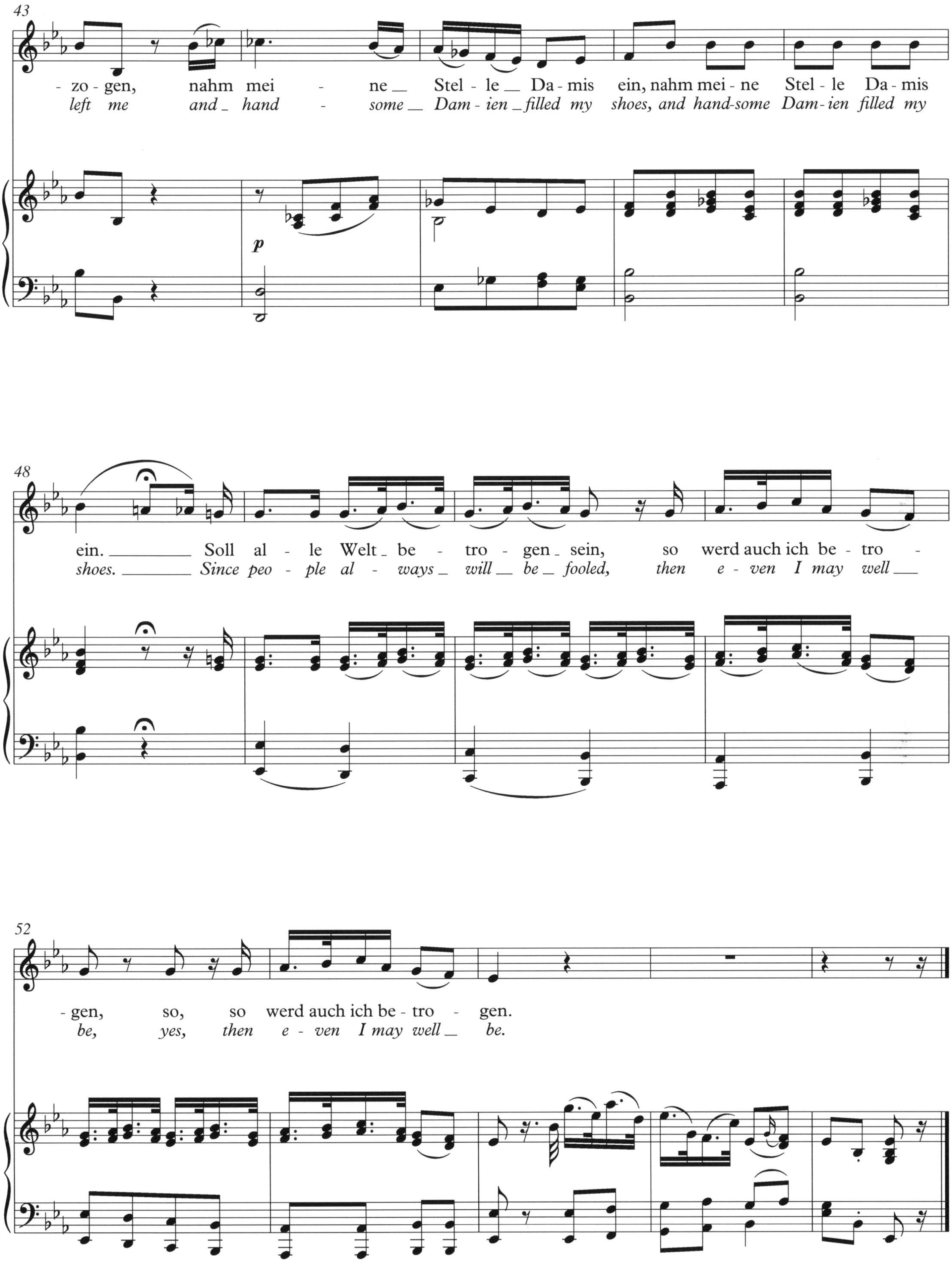
43
- zo - gen, nahm mei - ne Stel - le Da - mis ein, nahm mei - ne Stel - le Da - mis
left me and hand - some Dam - ien filled my shoes, and hand-some Dam - ien filled my
p
48
ein. Soll al - le Welt be - tro - gen sein, so werd auch ich be - tro -
shoes. Since peo - ple al - ways will be fooled, then e - ven I may well
52
- gen, so, so werd auch ich be - tro - gen.
be, yes, then e - ven I may well be.

# An Sylvia
## To Sylvia

Eduard von Bauernfeld (1802–1890), after
William Shakespeare

Franz Schubert (1797–1828)

range:

**Mässig** - *Moderate speed*

1. Was ist Sil - via, sa - get an, dass sie die wei - te Flur preist?
2. Ist sie schön und gut da - zu? Reiz labt sie wie mil - de Kind - heit;

*1. Who is Syl - via, what is she, that all our swains com - mend her?*
*2. Is she kind as she is fair? For beau - ty lives with kind - ness;*

Schön und zart seh
ih - rem Aug eilt
*Hol - y, fair and*
*to her eyes doth*

# Prinsessen
## Die Prinzessin
### *The Princess*

Bjørnsterne Bjørnson (1832–1910)  
Edvard Grieg (1843–1907)

**Allegretto semplice**

Prin - ses - sen sad højt i sit Jom - fru - bur. Smaa - gut - ten gik ne - de og blæ - ste paa Lur. "Hvi blæ - ser du al - tid, ti stil - le, du Smaa, det hæf - ter min Tan - ke, som vi - de vil gaa, nu naar Sol gaar ned, nu naar Sol gaar ned."

Es saß die Prin - zes - sin im Frau - en - ge - mach. Der Kna - be im Ta - le, er blies die Schal - mei. "Schweig stil - le, o Klei - ner, du fes - selst mir, ach! all' mei - ne Ge - dan - ken, die schweif - ten so frei, wenn die Son - ne sank, wenn die Son - ne sank."

*The prin - cess look'd down from her lof - ty height, a lad stood there play - ing in eve - ning's soft light. "O why must you blow on your horn, sil - ly boy, I want just to dream, and my thoughts you an - noy, as the sun goes down, as the sun goes down."*

# Trauer der Liebe
## Love's Sorrow

Johann Georg Jacobi (1740–1814)

Franz Schubert (1797–1828)

**Mäßig**

1. Wo die Taub' in stillen Buchen ihren Tauber sich erwählt, wo sich Nachtigallen suchen, und die Rebe sich vermählt; wo die Bäche sich vereinen, ging ich oft mit leichtem

2. O, da gab die finstre Laube leisen Trost im Abendschein; o, da kam ein süsser Glaube mit dem Morgenglanz im Hain; da vernahm ich's in den Winden, ihr Geflüster lehrte

1. *To the woods where, gently cooing, courting doves are wont to wait, where the nightingale goes wooing and the partridge finds its mate, I would go, alone and lonely, leave my merry life be-*

2. *How the twilit gloom consoled me, left abandoned and forlorn! How a sweet new hope enthralled me with the sun's first rays at dawn! And the wind itself was speaking in a whisper, just to*

# The Willow Song

William Shakespeare (1564–1616)

Arthur Sullivan (1842–1900)

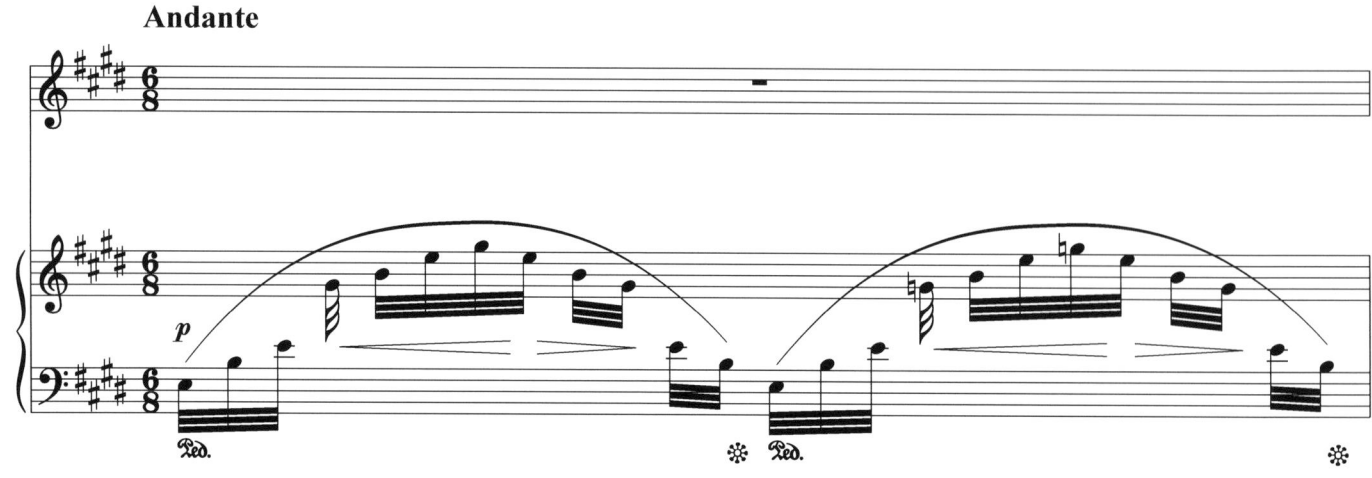

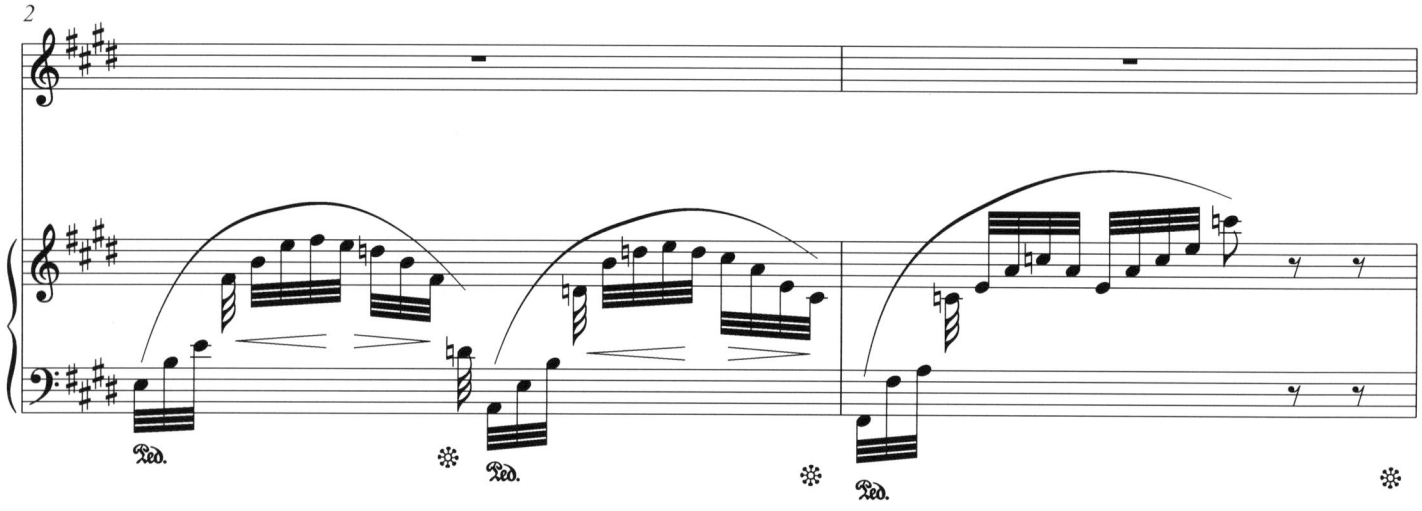

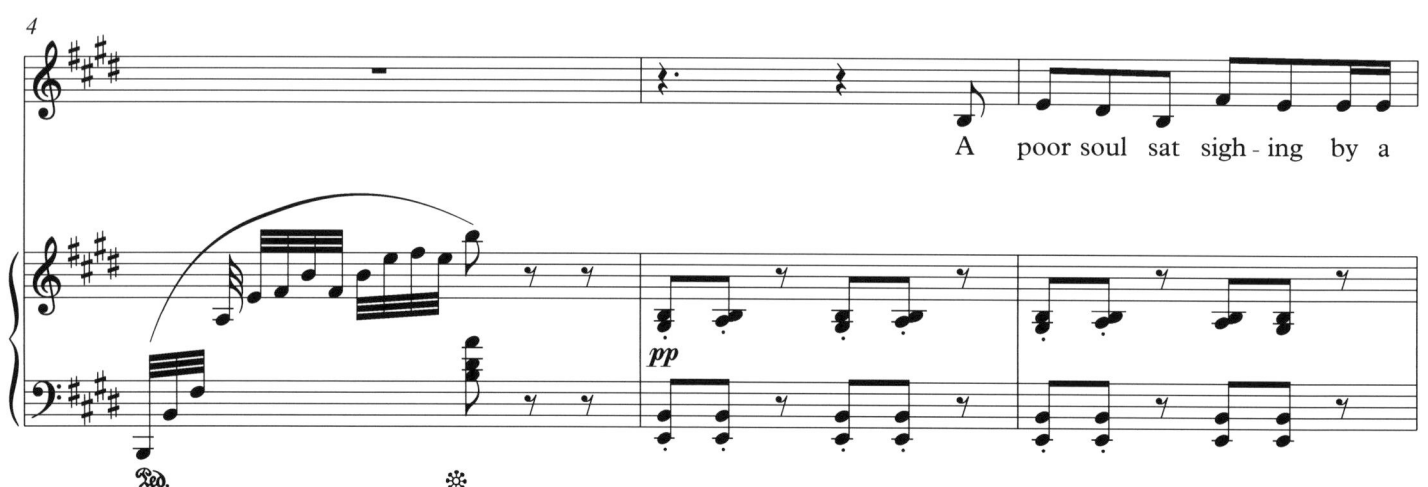

★ Composer's alternative

# When a felon's not engaged in his employment
## (The Policeman's Song)
### from *The Pirates of Penzance*

W. S. Gilbert (1836–1911)

Arthur Sullivan (1842–1900)

range:

# When a merry maiden marries
## from *The Gondoliers*

W. S. Gilbert (1836–1911)

Arthur Sullivan (1842–1900)

# Hinaus in's Freie!
## *Come Outside!*

August Heinrich Hoffmann von Fallersleben (1798–1874)

Robert Schumann (1810–1856)

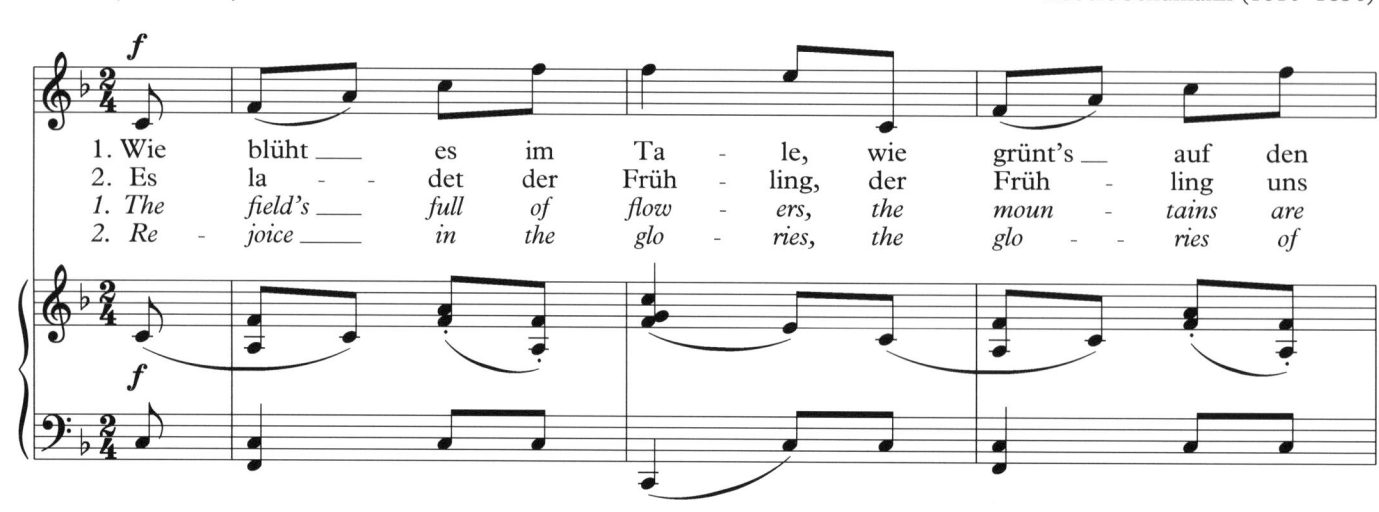

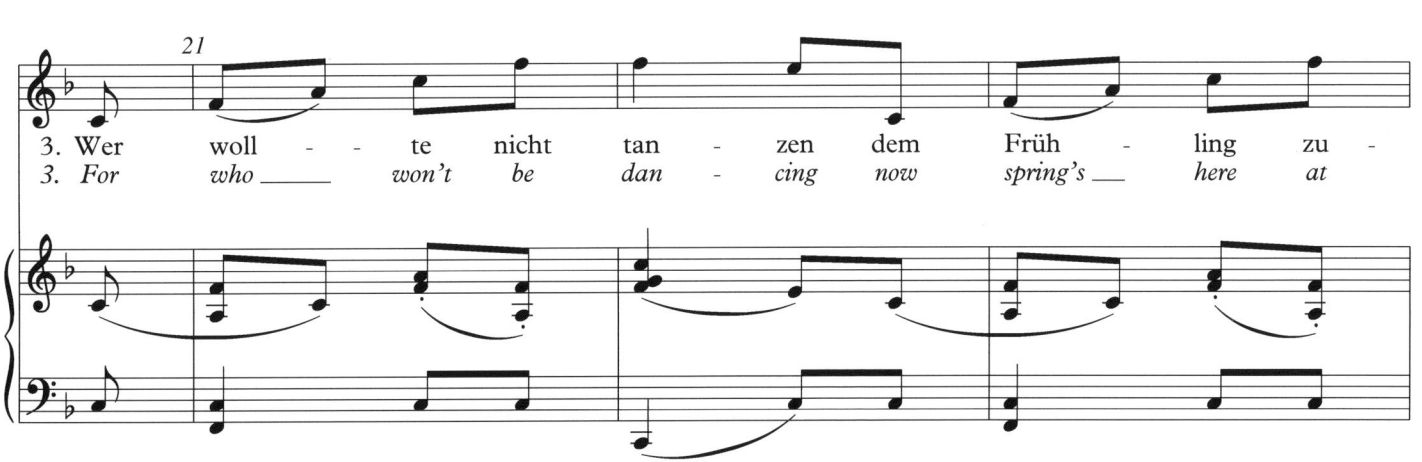